TCC South

Crowley Learning Center

CAREERS IN
PUBLIC LIBRARIES

HAVE YOU READ ANY GOOD BOOKS lately? If you are a librarian, you undoubtedly have, and you will probably never be at a loss for a good read. Being a librarian at a public library is more than shelving books and being able to recommend a good new novel. Librarians are curators of the written word and data in general. In public libraries those words and a seemingly endless amount of data are contained in everything from newspapers, magazines, and journals, to paperback and hardcover books of both nonfiction and fiction, as well as digital repositories of all kinds.

It is a librarian who, every day, leads people in all walks of life on a journey through all these resources. People rely on librarians to help them navigate the complicated world of technology, enabling everyone to maximize the wonders accessible in the public library.

For communities large and small throughout the United States, the public library is a major resource for literacy and education. Libraries serve people in a variety of ways, providing a quiet place to study and convenient tools for searching and applying for jobs. The librarian is the friendly face people seek out when entering this world of information.

The public library allows people to access millions of books, as well as audio recordings, movies, and other visual aids. Librarians are teachers, researchers, detectives, guides, guardians of knowledge, purveyors of information, skilled organizers, and problem solvers.

Millions of children have had their love for reading cultivated by a librarian who hosted a story hour at a local public library. Countless more children, with the aid of a librarian, have searched the shelves seeking out an exciting tale to spark their imagination.

Many children learned the basic skills needed to conduct research from librarians. It was a librarian who watched them go from elementary school through high school and college, using their research abilities to complete homework assignments and term papers.

Hunting down sources for people who are writing books or conducting research projects is where librarians put their talents as detectives to work. For many of these projects, the information needed is not easily found. That is when a librarian really gets tested, digging into the mounds of scholarly journals, papers, and letters left behind by generations, that may contain the answer to a baffling question, an unsolved problem, or a historical mystery.

Library science can open new worlds for people who enter the field. Each day presents an opportunity to research new topics you have never explored before, meet interesting people and touch many lives. This is also a career in public service, helping people retrieve information that might open a new chapter in their lives.

WHAT YOU CAN DO NOW

LEARN AS MUCH AS YOU CAN ABOUT ALL the services offered at public libraries near you. As a librarian, you will oversee those services and expand them, based on the community's needs.

In a recent national survey of Americans who use the public library, 20 percent said they were not aware of all the services their local public library offered. Take the opportunity to discover the full impact the public library has on your community, including offering free Internet services and informative lectures that help people learn more about federal programs like Social Security and Medicare. It will open your eyes to just how important public libraries are.

Volunteer at a public library. As a volunteer, you will do everything from shelve books to help patrons use technology, like computers and microfiche readers. You will get an opportunity to see the inner workings of the library firsthand and learn about all the tasks librarians undertake. As a library volunteer, you can get information and insight to help decide if a career in the library is for you. You can even volunteer at several different libraries and compare how things are done at a smaller library as opposed to a bigger one.

HISTORY OF THE PROFESSION

WHILE THE JOB DESCRIPTION FOR THE first librarians were not written in stone, some of the early texts they organized and preserved certainly were. Thousands of years ago, the Mesopotamians in the Ancient Near East reported and recorded the activities of the day on clay and stone tablets. In addition, literary texts, mathematical tables, dictionaries, historical accounts, and astronomical calculations were inscribed on these tablets. During the eighth century BC, these tablets began to mount up and even break, so the Assyrian king, Ashurbanipal, had an idea. He created a library in his palace in the Mesopotamian kingdom. He assigned a person, now considered one of the first librarians, as "the keeper of the tablets," to arrange all the inscribed tablets by subject.

Fortunately, being a librarian did not involve lugging heavy tablets around when Gabriel Naude, one of the world's most noted librarians, started his career in 1622. Born in Paris in 1600, roughly 160 years after the printing press was invented, Naude was fascinated by books and the knowledge and information contained in them. Naude wrote his first book in 1620. It was a commentary on politics in France at the time. The president of the Paris Parliament, Henri de Mesmes, read Naude's book and was impressed by it. He was also aware of Naude's scholarly interests. With that in mind, Mesmes asked Naude to become his personal librarian. Mesmes had more than 8,000 books in his library. While working for the president of the Paris

Parliament, Naude learned a great deal about building and maintaining a library. He believed a library should be filled with works both ancient and modern, written by well-known as well as obscure authors. He also devised what was considered the first cataloging system.

Based on detailed notes he took about his experiences as a librarian for Mesmes, Naude wrote a book called *Advice on Establishing a Library*, which he completed in 1627. The book is considered the first great work on library science and it is still read by many people in the field today.

Naude went on to become the librarian for Cardinal Jules Mazarin in 1642 and helped establish the renowned Bibliotheque Mazarine in Paris. That library was opened to the public in 1643, making it the oldest public library in France and one of the oldest in the world.

The concept of opening libraries to the public and lending out books was a novel idea. Most libraries of the period were not lending libraries and not open to the public. For example, wealthy people who could afford to amass large collections of books had private libraries in their estates with thousands of volumes for their personal use. Religious and educational institutions also had libraries, but only people affiliated with those groups could use those libraries. All these repositories of books had librarians to organize their volumes.

By the late 17th century, public libraries were being established throughout Europe and the idea was gaining acceptance in the American Colonies as well. The forerunner to the public library in the New World was subscription libraries. These libraries had dues-paying members. The dues covered the cost of buying new books, and only members could borrow the books. The statesman Benjamin Franklin and several of his friends started the first subscription library in the Colonies in 1731. Called the Library Company of Philadelphia, Franklin was its first librarian and catalogued all the books.

Subscription libraries eventually gave way to free public libraries, open to the public, with a varied array of books, and librarians in charge of the reading material. In 1743, residents of Darby, Pennsylvania decided to start a public lending library and each of the 29 founders contributed money to buy books. John Pearson, a leather-worker and leading local citizen, was elected the first librarian and the books were kept in his home.

When the residents of an Eastern Massachusetts community voted in 1778 to name their town Franklin after Benjamin Franklin, the esteemed statesman donated more than one hundred books to the municipality. The townspeople decided to establish a library and lend the books out, under the supervision of a librarian, but only to Franklin residents. When the public library in Peterborough, New Hampshire was started in 1833, it was supported by taxpayers' dollars, the first library to be funded that way. The money was used to buy books and pay a librarian.

Librarianship got a big boost when Melville Dewey entered the profession in 1873. He is the best-known librarian ever and is considered the father of modern American librarianship. While working at the Amherst College Library, Dewey, who had always been obsessed with order, became frustrated with what he thought was the illogical way books in the library were arranged. A student at the college, Dewey made a proposal to the faculty to implement a new system he had developed to arrange holdings in the library. Using decimals, Dewey developed an easy, uniform system to catalog and organize materials in the library. Intrigued by the method Dewey devised, the faculty allowed him to put the system in place to reorganize the library. Dewey's master plan worked wonderfully.

In 1876, the young librarian wrote a pamphlet explaining his new system. Soon librarians all over the country were implementing the Dewey Decimal System in their libraries, and it continues to be used today. Dewey attended the Convention of Librarians, held during the Centennial Exposition in Philadelphia in October 1876. With 103 librarians in attendance, Dewey saw an opportunity to channel the enthusiasm these people had for books and learning into a strong voice for the profession. He helped found the American Library Association (ALA) at the convention.

A year later Dewey became one of the founders and the first editor of the influential Library Journal. When Dewey became head librarian at Columbia College in New York City in 1883, he proposed establishing the first school to train librarians. The School of Library Economy was started at Columbia in 1884 with Dewey in charge.

At around the same time that Dewey was bolstering the librarian profession, steel magnate and multimillionaire Andrew Carnegie was offering grants to communities willing to build libraries. Additional libraries meant more jobs for librarians. Between 1883 and 1919, money donated by Carnegie was used to build roughly 1,689 libraries, a majority of them public libraries.

More colleges throughout the nation began teaching library science, and the ALA was a leading force in standardizing the curriculum at these colleges. As libraries continued to grow in the 20th century, they became more than just a place to house a collection of books. Libraries were developing into information and cultural centers.

Advances in technology, especially over the last 60 years, have had a great impact on libraries and librarianship in general. Now librarians can use computers to help patrons conduct wide-ranging, in-depth research, and track down information that would have been very difficult to find decades ago. The role of the librarian continues to grow as libraries throughout the nation expand services to meet the needs of patrons in this technologically advanced and information-driven society.

WHERE YOU WILL WORK

PUBLIC LIBRARIES COME IN ALL SHAPES AND SIZES, giving librarians a wide range of options when it comes to choosing a workplace. There are more than 16,000 small, medium, large, and even enormous public libraries (when branches are included in the count) in urban, suburban, and rural areas across the country.

Large public libraries have voluminous collections, with much more room to house the latest equipment and store archival material. Smaller libraries, on the other hand, tend to be quaint, low-key, and more personal. Computers help bridge the gap in terms of shelf space. You can work in a small library and still access digital copies of materials that your patrons need.

Large libraries in bustling urban areas have heavy foot traffic, and that creates a more harried atmosphere for librarians. The staffs at these libraries are bigger, but because there are so many patrons to serve, the demands on a librarian's time can make for a stressful workplace. In addition, people who live and work in large urban areas, like New York City, Boston, Washington, Chicago, and Los Angeles, are used to having things done for them immediately, and that makes the librarian's job somewhat hectic. However, because you are in the middle of a city, you can bring in famous authors and offer an array of literary programs.

A regional library in a suburban setting may serve several large communities or a few counties. These libraries can be just as sizable in terms of square footage as a big urban library, but the pace is somewhat slower.

Many small towns have medium-sized libraries with most of the latest reads, some of the more popular periodicals, computers, e-books, copy machines, and a meeting room to host lectures and movie nights. Much appreciated by their patrons, librarians figure prominently in the community because the library plays such an important role in the town.

There are small libraries that serve towns of as few as 500 people. Located in historic houses or buildings, these libraries have all the charm and warmth of a town right out of a Jessica Fletcher novel, and librarians who work in these easygoing bastions of books are usually on a first-name basis with their patrons. Libraries in resort areas often feature books about the local history and resources, and the librarian may serve as an informal travel guide to visitors.

There are also various departments in most libraries. For instance, you might be a children's librarian. In the children's department, imagination abounds and your workplace is surrounded by wondrous stuffed animals, vibrant colors, posters, and other accouterments to make the library a fun place for youngsters. You might work in the reference department, surrounded by the tools necessary to answer the most obscure questions that come your way.

Whether you are working in a modern architectural marvel, a library building that has become an enduring landmark, or a historic home, you would have to admit that yours is one of the most interesting work environments around.

THE WORK YOU WILL DO

"GOOGLE CAN BRING YOU BACK 100,000 answers. A librarian can bring you back the right one," British author Neil Gaiman once said. That is the most important part of the work you do as a librarian, giving people the most precise, up-to-date, and authoritative answer to their queries. Every time you assist a patron, you put your reputation on the line, because not just any answer will do – only the correct one. So that means a librarian's job goes on behind the scenes, as you work to stay on top of the latest cutting-edge developments in library and information science. That goes for both technological advances and new sources of information.

When it comes to tracking down data, public librarians have to know where to look and what tools are the best to use to conduct the search. A complete working knowledge of the holdings in the public library you work in is paramount. You are in the information business and you must know your inventory. If you do not have what the patron needs, Plan B is directing the person to another library that can offer that needed information or resources.

Sometimes the public library is the only way for people to obtain the information they need. You are helping people break down barriers, giving them access to facts, figures, documents, services, photographs, and other resources. Today's librarians are in the unique position of combining their traditional duties – giving patrons access to books, periodicals, and printed research materials – with the latest technological media.

When librarians come to work, they are responsible for getting the library up and running. Computers, printers, and copy machines have to be turned on, and librarians have to make sure all the library equipment is working properly before patrons start entering the building.

Throughout the day, librarians maintain order in the library, and that does not mean making sure everyone speaks in whispers. No one likes to see a library in disarray, with books and magazines piling up here and there, cluttering the building. So librarians are on their feet all day, grabbing books and periodicals off tables and chairs and shelving them for the next patron to use. It all comes down to organization. Librarians make sure books, documents, publications, reference materials, and audiovisual aids are easily and readily accessible for both patrons and staff.

Part of your job is to read announcements about upcoming titles and be alert to the latest nonfiction and literary trends. You have to keep up with book reviews and be well versed in what is moving up on the best-seller lists.

Librarians handle voluminous amounts of material each day as public library collections continue to grow from books to all types of advanced media, like audio books, DVDs, e-books, and e-readers. Some libraries even lend out jigsaw puzzles, games, and artwork.

There are three basic areas of library work: user services, technical services, and administrative services. In larger public libraries, a staff of librarians can divide up these tasks, but in a smaller public library only one or two librarians on staff will manage library services, oversee administration, and meet patron needs. In many communities, librarians spread the word through local newspapers and other news media about all the services and programs available at the library.

Most libraries have a Head Librarian and larger repositories even employ an Assistant or Associate Head Librarian. Head Librarians oversee the public library staff, which includes volunteers, as well as the entire library operation.

The biggest part of the administrative job is preparing an annual budget and then staying within that budget. Since public libraries are funded through municipal or county budgets, the amount of money available to subsidize the library changes from year to year. At times, there may be drastic cutbacks and, in any year, there usually is not enough money available in the budget to provide the library with the amount of funding librarians feel is necessary.

Staying within budgetary constraints, while keeping the library at the forefront of technological advances and the most recently released reading material, can be quite a balancing act. This is where knowing your patrons is vital, as well as having some insight into what other libraries around you have in their collections.

For example, you may decide to purchase more books and periodicals than computers because a nearby library has the money to buy computers and lets people from your community use them. So you have fewer computers, but more printed reading material, which is affordable within your budget. As Head Librarian, you are going to have to make some tough decisions about what you can acquire.

Staffing is another concern. Patrons are looking for assistance and you need enough people on the staff to provide it, but the salaries to pay staff members must fit within your budget and will test your priorities regarding what is most important – library holdings, equipment, or personnel. It is your job to keep an open line of communication with elected officials and local government administration. To get the funding you need, you need to keep members of the town council or the county legislature informed of the variety of services the library provides taxpayers and the high dividends the municipality gets from that money.

Public libraries usually have library boards and you will have to work with board members in your job. In most cases, library board trustees are appointed to the board by elected officials. The good news is that these people are usually tireless advocates for the library. They are determined that the library be able to fulfill its mission. Trustees often find ways to increase budgets for the library and, through the work of the American Library Association, have become vocal allies for librarians.

Another aspect of your job is working with a group of volunteers, usually called Friends of the Library. If you are lucky, your library has one of these groups, which helps with fundraising and increasing public awareness of the library. Oftentimes, these groups raise enough money to buy additional books and equipment for the public library that is not covered by the budget. Librarians play an important role in integrating these volunteers into the library infrastructure, building their enthusiasm, making them part of the team, letting them know what the library needs and why, and making sure these volunteers get the recognition they deserve from the library staff and patrons for the good work they do.

Often overlooked is the public librarian's work as an educator. In years past, librarians would teach people how to use the Dewey Decimal System, the card catalog, and printed directories to find materials in the library. Today, librarians also have to teach people how to use all the new technology. You are going to spend a substantial part of your day teaching people of all ages how to use these devices. In addition, you will be introducing patrons to methods used to access numerous online databases and virtual libraries.

The public library serves as a center of cultural activities and other special events. The Head Librarian comes up with ideas for programs and activities to be hosted by the library. These programs have to appeal to a wide spectrum of people, from book discussion groups and movie nights, to music and dance programs, to lectures and demonstrations about yoga and healthy eating.

No matter how big a public library building is, there is only so much room on the library shelves, so as new material comes in, especially books, librarians have to determine which books, periodicals, and other materials have to be taken out of circulation. Librarians spend hours poring over their circulation statistics to see what types of books and what overall subject categories have had robust circulation numbers over the past few years. Taking materials out of circulation is always a difficult decision.

The same is true with acquisitions. Decisions about what materials to get for the library are never taken lightly and consume much of a librarian's time. Acquisitions are an ongoing process. New books are coming out all the time and patrons expect their library to have all the hottest best sellers as well as other books of note.

Large libraries have an Acquisitions Librarian just to handle this important ongoing task. Becoming an Acquisitions Librarian is just one area of specialization for librarians. Acquisitions Librarians procure both print and non-print materials (DVDs, CDs, etc.), and deal with the suppliers of those materials. Being familiar with the needs and tastes of your patrons is a requirement for an Acquisitions Librarian.

Another area of specialization in public libraries is the job of the Reference Librarian. Reference Librarians handle the multitude of research requests coming from patrons. The Reference Librarian has to make the quickest transition to the fast-changing technology and be conversant with the newest databases.

Planning, organizing, and overseeing the use of media resources falls to the Media Librarian in large libraries. The Media Librarian teaches patrons how to use this equipment and makes sure it is well maintained and not abused by anyone. The Media Librarian also must be aware of the newest library media equipment on the market and determine if the equipment the library already has is meeting the needs of its patrons.

Children's Librarians help introduce youngsters to the joys of reading. No child is too young to use the children's section in the library, and Children's Librarians have to know how to work with youngsters of all ages. Making reading fun and the library an enjoyable place to visit are jobs for the Children's Librarian. Developing an ongoing program of special events, such as scavenger hunts, sing-a-longs, and mommy and me arts and crafts programs, is also an integral part of your job.

When children enter their teen years, the Young Adult Librarian will help them reach their next level of reading and introduce them to the growing number of books specially written for teenagers.

The larger the library, the greater the opportunity that various tasks will be broken down into areas of specialization. This gives librarians the chance to focus on one area of library science that interests them the most.

LIBRARIANS TELL THEIR OWN STORIES

I Am the Head Librarian at a Public Library

"Head librarians basically oversee the entire library operation. The job entails everything from ordering books, to training and supervising personnel, to drawing up a budget.

There's a great deal of work involved in this job, and some of the administrative tasks take me off the library floor and away from interacting with patrons. To me that's a bit of a drawback, since I became a librarian because I enjoy working with people and helping them discover all the wonders of the library. I'm a people person and I'd much rather be assisting patrons than sitting behind a desk crunching numbers and managing the budget.

You really have to know your community and your patrons. Every library is different and has different needs. For instance, you may have disabled people who use your library and need special equipment, like a Pearl Reader (designed for people who are blind). That was high on the list of equipment I pushed hard to get when I became the head librarian. I knew we had patrons who would rely on it and use it on a regular basis. It was money well spent. It made us a more accessible and caring library.

You may have senior citizens who would benefit from large-type books, or you might have a younger community that has a greater need for books for children and young adults. Successful librarians take the time to talk to patrons and listen to their ideas and suggestions. This gives you insight into what your community needs, wants, and will support. Then you plan accordingly, putting your resources where they will be of most benefit.

When a library serves the needs of its patrons, it gains their support as well. As a public library we get most of our funds from the town council. When council members hear voters sing our praises, we are more likely to get the funds we need to continue to operate at full capacity. I never miss an opportunity to tell council members about what's happening at the library. Elected officials must understand that the money they give the library is being put to good use every day. Council members have to be aware of everything the library and its staff do all year long. I want council members to know how important we are to the community, so the library is not the first thing that comes to mind when there have to be municipal budget cuts, but instead the library is the program the council won't ever cut.

I'm an advocate for the public library – there's no doubt about that. I know where the community would be without it. So many people use it. Our library is an educational, cultural, and informational institution, as well as an irreplaceable resource."

I Am a Research Librarian at a Large Public Library

"I think this is the best job a librarian can have. I never know what to expect, what people might want to research today. It might be a homework assignment, someone looking up information about a health issue, or, as I had the other day, a woman doing research for a mystery novel she was writing. The job never gets boring and I am always learning new things.

Patrons come up to my desk and say, 'Have you ever heard of . . . ?' And after 17 years on this job, usually I can say to their amazement, yes, and I know a shortcut I can take to start researching the information they need. I'm a problem solver, finding ways to quickly get people the data they need or at least get them started on their way to a fruitful search. It's like solving a puzzle or, when someone is searching for something really tough, cracking a mystery.

We help people who come in the library to conduct a search as well as people who call us on the phone and email us. People who really don't know what a research librarian does all day are amazed when they hear what my day is like, the amount of work we have, and how much we get accomplished. We are not here to do the work for people, just to set them on the right track and help if they get stuck along the way. Our goal is to assist as many people as we possibly can, do it as quickly as possible, yet be attentive and, most important, be accurate. This is public service at its best.

Think about it: Where else can people go to get this information? It's free and priceless at the same time. It's very rewarding when you get that look of astonishment on someone's face or hear the excitement in their voice when you tell them you found something or can give them a valuable lead. I can't tell you how many times I've heard 'Wow! How'd you find that?' "

I Am a Children's Librarian at a Public Library

"When it comes to getting children to develop a love for reading, I am on the front lines. That means children must have a positive experience every time they come to the library. I want to make sure children who come to the public library ask their parents to bring them back. I want the public library to be one of the go-to places when kids go out. My goal is to have kids borrow books, read them, bring those books back, and get more books.

Most public library children's departments work with kids through the sixth grade, or about age twelve. Some children's departments go to fourteen years old. It has to do with reading level as well. Children can come here and use the children's department and the computers at this library at any age.

If a child needs a book in the young adult department, we are happy to help find it. If a child is more comfortable making a gradual transition from the children's department to the adult library, that's fine. Just as I want to help young children discover the joys of reading in the first place, I want to assist those children in their journey to young adult books and beyond. I have a chance to develop a lifelong patron for the public library and I'm determined to do that.

This job makes you happy. Something cute and fun happens almost every day. You work in a cheerful, relaxed environment. We try to make the children's department as stimulating and exciting as possible. We change things around, so kids see something new all the time. There are always different books on display, so youngsters can pick up the books and look through them. It's very hands-on – part reading room, part playground for the mind.

We want a visit here to be a fun outing for parents as well. Children's librarians need parents to be involved in this process. We may spark an interest in reading but parents have to fan the flames. We are allies in this, so I always welcome input and participation from the parents.

When children love to read, they can't wait to come to the library. You become a trusted friend to these youngsters and you get a chance to introduce them to so many new friends through the characters in the books we have. You can see imagination come alive.

Like most libraries, we offer a story hour and I think that's a children's librarian's favorite time of day. We not only read to the children, but we bring the books and characters to life and hopefully pique these youngsters' interest enough that they want their parents to read to them and, more importantly, they want to be able to read the books for themselves. I think we are teaching them how valuable reading is and how many books they can have at their fingertips by coming to the public library.

The books that are read during story hour are very carefully chosen. We want books that teach valuable lessons, books that are thought provoking, that kids will talk about with their parents, siblings, and friends. I want to read stories to these children that will stay with them. So children's librarians are always searching for these kinds of books.

As a children's librarian, you have to keep up on the latest books released for kids in the various age groups, as well as knowing which old standards to bring back time and again because the kids love them so much. I love when young parents come to my department with their children and say with a big smile, 'This was one of my favorite places growing up.' That means we did our job."

PERSONAL QUALIFICATIONS

IN A LIBRARY, EVERY ONE OF THE THOUSANDS of items in the collection has its place. That is how patrons, as well as librarians, are able to find things. Librarians must have superior organizational skills. They do not put books down and never get around to shelving them, set aside files and fail to put them away, or forget to bring a periodical back to its rightful place on a display rack.

Librarians are also detail oriented. Nothing can be overlooked. No detail is too small when it is your job to keep the library running smoothly. Having a good memory helps. Knowing exactly where to look for something gives patrons a sense of confidence when turning to you for assistance.

A love for books and research is a must. Successful librarians never let their talent for tracking down hard-to-find information diminish. Having a gift for evaluating resources and determining which stand out are essential to this career.

Very high on the list of qualifications for librarians today are technical skills. Technology is a big part of the job and you have to be an expert in it, at least in the technology used in the library field. You can never stop learning how to use all the new technology that is continually introduced to put libraries on the cutting edge of the research and information world. Feeling comfortable working with this technology is mandatory.

The career also involves showing patrons how to use the latest technology. Librarians always have to be patient, but especially when it comes to teaching people how to use complicated new technology. You may have to give patrons tutorials on how to use the newest devices until they get the hang of it. Patrons want to use this equipment, even though they may be far from tech-savvy. So, add teaching to your professional duties.

The ability to communicate well is a must. That allows you to connect with your patrons, figure out what they want, explain to them the resources the library has and how you can help them. Being a good listener is another key trait. You are working in a public library and you are serving members of the community at large. Librarians have to enjoy being around people and assisting them all day long. People have come to expect a friendly, warm, and helpful reception when they approach a librarian. So, even at times when patrons ask for the impossible, you stay cool, calm, and collected.

ATTRACTIVE FEATURES

A LIBRARY IS A WONDERFUL PLACE TO WORK. It is quiet and serene, conducive to getting work done. You never have to wander very far to find a peaceful place to gather your thoughts (or read a book).

Being surrounded by books is a delightful backdrop to any workplace, and many public libraries have courtyards and gardens that provide a convenient and tranquil place to take in some fresh air during breaks. Most public libraries also have rotating exhibits, so there is constantly something new and interesting to check out during the workday, and art usually adorns the walls. Libraries are designed and decorated to be welcoming and relaxing places for people to come to and spend time in, and librarians enjoy that environment, too.

Everyone who works in a public library shares a love for books, so you will have much in common with your coworkers. Those mutual interests cultivate teamwork in the workplace. Librarians are always more than willing to pass along to their colleagues what they have learned about new sources of information, research tools, and shortcuts for finding data. This builds camaraderie within the library staff and results in a cooperative effort that makes everyone's job easier.

As a librarian, you have your finger on the pulse of the publishing world.

You keep up with the latest books being released, new authors bursting on the scene, and literary trends. You will come across all kinds of books you probably would have never known about or sought out if you did not work in a library. Not every fascinating book makes it to a top 10 list, a summer reading list, or a best-seller list. Some extremely worthwhile books escape the attention of critics and reviewers. Few of these gems get past librarians, who really know what is in their library's collections, and they can introduce these volumes to readers looking for page-turners they never expected to find.

A librarian's recommendations about books are eagerly sought out by library patrons and the librarian's opinion is well-respected. You are considered an expert in what you do by the people who come to you for assistance, and that is a good feeling. In this rewarding job you interact with all kinds of people. You help patrons ranging in age from toddlers to senior citizens.

New technology is always being introduced in libraries. This keeps you on the cutting edge of innovative advances in information gathering, storage, and retrieval.

Librarians have a host of transferable skills that are valuable in other fields besides library work. Chief among them are research and organizational skills, but critical thinking, expertise in communications, working well with a wide range of people, being knowledgeable in a variety of subjects, and numerous other traits give you marketable talents if you ever need or want to make a career change.

There are plenty of opportunities to be creative in your job. As a librarian, you want to draw people into the library, especially those who are not frequent library visitors, so they can see everything the facility has to offer and make use of it. You do this by coming up with imaginative programs, such as cooking classes, puppet shows, talks by authors, reading groups, and concerts. These programs pique the interest of members of the community of all ages, get them into the library, allowing them to see all what is going on, and, hopefully, turn them into library regulars.

UNATTRACTIVE ASPECTS

TECHNOLOGY IS GREAT WHEN IT IS WORKING, but when it is not, it can cause a librarian big headaches. Trying to figure out what is wrong with a computer, printer, microfiche reader, Internet connection, or copy machine – especially when people are anxiously waiting to use it – is aggravating for everyone. At times, a repair cannot be made without calling in tech support from outside the public library system. That may take hours, even days. Up go those signs asking people to forgive the inconvenience and thanking them for their patience. It is not your fault if the equipment does not work, although you will get blamed for it.

Some patrons are just plain rude. Nothing you do is fast enough or good enough for them. It does not happen often because a vast majority of library patrons truly appreciate everything you do. Every once in a while you cross paths with an ill-mannered patron. In those cases, you must have thick skin, try to defuse the situation, and handle the surly patron's concern as quickly as possible so you can move on to helping patrons who value the service you provide.

As a librarian, you are not working on a nine-to-five schedule. Libraries generally open early, and most stay open late into the evening and are open on weekends. You work irregular hours, and that can cut into your social life and time with your family.

Public libraries are funded by taxpayer dollars, mostly from the municipalities and counties where the libraries are located. Financial support may also come from local donations and fundraising events as well, but that can be inconsistent. Budgets for public libraries are always tight. They can fluctuate from year to year and are often subject to cuts. Unfortunately, when elected officials allocate money to public libraries, those decisions are rarely based on much study of library use or even needs. Consequently, the library may be shortchanged, and that means librarians have to work within a budget that simply does not provide enough funds to replace worn-out equipment or buy many of the most popular and sought-after books. Sometimes budget constraints lead to library staff layoffs and pay cuts.

EDUCATION AND TRAINING

A MASTER OF LIBRARY SCIENCE (MLS) DEGREE or a Master of Library and Information Science (MLIS) degree is usually required. An applicant who does not have an MLS or an MLIS is rarely hired as a librarian.

An undergraduate degree in library and/or information science is not a prerequisite to enter an MLS or MLIS program. Only a small number of colleges even offer a bachelor's degree in these majors. That is because hiring practices in the library field dictate that librarians have a master's level degree. An undergraduate degree will only get you a support staff position in a public library.

For the most part, students who pursue an MLS or an MLIS degree can major in any subject they want as undergraduates, though many opt to get bachelor's degrees in English, history, computer science, or communications. However, an undergraduate degree in library and/or information science is a good stepping-stone to an MLS or an MLIS.

The University of Southern Mississippi in Hattiesburg is one of the few colleges in the nation where students can earn a bachelor's degree in library and information science. Courses in Reference and Information Service, Library Management, Media Utilization, and Special Problems in Librarianship, as well as Cataloging and Classification, are all part of the program. Students can do their graduate work at the university and earn an MLIS.

A bachelor's degree in information management and services is offered at Southern Connecticut State University in New Haven. This course of study focuses on a variety of library-related skills, primarily in the research area. A concentration on computer skills specific to the information services field is also available.

The University of North Texas in Denton has designed a wide-ranging bachelor's degree program in information science. It includes courses on Information Architecture, Information Management, Digital Content, and Information Organization. The University of North Texas also has a master's of library science and a doctoral program in information science.

There are more than 60 colleges and universities in the United States and Canada with MLS and MLIS programs that have been accredited by the American Library Association (ALA). Libraries prefer to hire librarians with MLS or MLIS degrees from an ALA-accredited school.

It is worth taking the time to research each of the schools you are interested in when it comes to getting your MLS or MLIS, because each one has its own areas of specialization. For example, the MLIS program at Louisiana State University in Baton Rouge offers specializations in Adult Services in Public Libraries, Youth Services Librarianship, School Librarianship, Digital Content Management, and several others.

At the University of Pittsburgh, specializations range from Archives and Information Science, Information Technology, and Resources and Services: Children and Youth.

The primary areas of MLIS specialization at Wayne State University in Detroit include Library Services, Information Management, and Archives and Digital Content Management.

Rare Books and Manuscripts, Music Librarianship, and Children's and Young Adult Services are tracks in the MLS program at Indiana University, Bloomington.

Some of these schools put more of an emphasis on an area of librarianship that you are interested in. That is why it is good to check out each program carefully. A number of universities, like the University of Buffalo (New York), offer ALA-accredited MLS or MLIS degrees online.

Most employers look favorably on candidates with MLS or MLIS degrees received online from reputable universities. These employers are generally impressed that candidates had the technical skills needed to complete an online degree in library and/or information science.

In some states, public librarians must be certified. The process usually requires the librarian to have an MLS or an MLIS degree from an ALA-accredited school. In certain states, like New Mexico, librarians have to take a test to be certified. The rules for certification vary from state to state and if you move from one state to another you will have to get certification from the new state in order to work in a public library there. These certifications are not reciprocal from one state to another.

EARNINGS

SALARIES GENERALLY DEPEND ON THE size of the public library and its location. Librarians in big urban areas who work for large public library systems make more money than those with jobs in small libraries in rural areas. In addition, your experience and the type of responsibilities you have are also among the considerations that go into determining pay scales.

Another variable regarding paychecks for those working in a public library is the wealth of the community. A town with a robust tax base and a budget that meets all its needs can offer higher salaries to its librarians than a town struggling to pay for the basics.

With those factors in mind, national statistics show that the median annual salary for public librarians is about $50,000. In New York City the median yearly income for librarians employed in a public library is almost $70,000, in Los Angeles it is $65,000, and Chicago reports $62,000.

Starting salaries in urban areas are about $40,000 for librarians and can go up to well over $100,000, depending on job title, such as head children's librarian or librarian media specialist. Many large libraries offer full benefits, including healthcare and retirement packages. Keep in mind that librarians in large library systems are often represented by unions and that results in higher pay and better benefits.

The pay scale in rural areas can start in the $25,000 range and go up to $65,000 for head librarians. Benefits may vary greatly in these regions, but usually include health insurance of some type. The cost of living in rural communities is also lower.

OPPORTUNITIES

JOB GROWTH FOR LIBRARIANS IS ON THE rebound, recovering from a slowdown several years ago. Experts are projecting that jobs for librarians will grow at a rate of almost eight percent over the next 10 years.

At one time, it was thought that with all the new technology, including the Internet, people would no longer need public libraries. Nothing could be further from the truth, as people continue to use public libraries in record numbers. In fact, the new technology has prompted people to go to the library even more than before.

Those who cannot afford a computer in their home or simply cannot keep up with all the technological advances, such as expensive software programs, are turning to the library for assistance. At the public library, people can use computers for free and get aid from knowledgeable librarians on how to use the latest technology to track down information.

With more patrons, libraries need more librarians. These repositories of information keep evolving to meet the needs of the community and that translates into more jobs for librarians.

As the price of books continues to spiral upwards, people turn to their local public library where they can borrow the latest page-turners free of charge. While public libraries are funded by taxpayer dollars, and government budgets are always tenuous, elected officials see all the foot traffic at local public libraries and realize that the expenditure to keep these facilities open is money well spent.

If you are looking for opportunities in the library field, one of your first stops should be the job board at the American Library Association's website. In addition, all 50 states have library associations, and there are also regional library associations, such as the Mountain Plains Library Association (MPLA), the New England Library Association (NELA), the Pacific Northwest Library Association (PNLA), and the Southeastern Library Association (SELA), among others. Most of these associations have very up-to-date job boards on their websites with positions that need to be filled quickly.

In addition, opportunities for advancement abound in this field. Librarians can move up to assistant library director or library director. Those promotions come with a pay hike. Many library boards like to pick their management teams from within, preferring people who not only know the library, the library staff, and the volunteers, but the patrons and the needs of the community as well. There is no learning curve when you promote a librarian from your system to assistant director or director of the library, as there often is when outsiders are brought in to fill those jobs. Library board members also feel that people who have served the community as librarians understand the budgetary constraints faced by the public library they serve and, in management positions, will know how to get the most out of every dollar spent.

GETTING STARTED

TAKE THE TIME TO GET TO KNOW SOME librarians in your area. They can be an excellent resource, both as mentors and references. Each of them has a story about how they got started in a specific career, and an established librarian can give you valuable insights about how to break into the library field.

Clerical staff and technicians who do supportive jobs for the library, such as running the bookmobile, help the library keep meeting the patrons' needs. It will not be the job title you hoped for or the salary you wanted, but it will give you entree into the field. From there you can move up or move on, but you are working in your chosen field. Most important, you are gaining experience, and that is something future employers will look for.

You need to be flexible. Take an entry-level job, consider accepting a lower salary, and think about relocating to get your dream job. In addition, do not rule out part-time work or taking a temporary position at a public library. These jobs give you a chance to showcase your talents and can lead to a full-time job. Besides, it helps build a résumé, gets you out in the field, and shows potential employers that you are committed to doing what it takes.

Join library associations around the country, including the American Library Association (ALA) – one of its divisions is the Public Library Association. All of them welcome students. Attend the meetings and conferences held by these groups. There you can make valuable contacts in the field.

ASSOCIATIONS

■ **Public Library Association (PLA)**
http://www.ala.org/pla

■ **American Library Association (ALA)**
http://www.ala.org

■ **Association for Rural and Small Libraries (ARSL)**
http://arsl.info

■ **Council on Library and Information Resources (CLIR)**
http://www.clir.org

■ Association for Library and Information Science Education (ALISE)
http://www.alise.org

■ Association for Library Service to Children (ALSC)
http://www.ala.org/alsc

■ National Association to Promote Library & Information Services to Latinos and the Spanish Speaking (REFORMA)
http://www.reforma.org

■ International Federation of Library Associations and Institutions (IFLA)
http://www.ifla.org

PERIODICALS

Library Journal
American Libraries Magazine
Computers in Libraries
Children & Libraries
Library Quarterly
Public Library Quarterly
Public Libraries
Library Technology Report
Information Technology and Libraries
Information Standards Quarterly
Publishers Weekly
Smart Libraries Newsletter

WEBSITES

■ Public Libraries Online
http://publiclibrariesonline.org

■ Urban Libraries Council (ULC)
http://www.urbanlibraries.org

■ Library Stuff
http://www.librarystuff.net

■ Librarian.net
http://www.librarian.net

- **United for Libraries**
  http://www.ala.org/united

- **PublicLibraries.com**
  http://www.publiclibraries.com

- **Library Spot**
  http://www.libraryspot.com

- **Institute of Museum and Library Services (IMLS)**
  https://www.imls.gov

- **State and Regional Library Association List**
  www.ala.org/groups/affiliates/chapters/state/stateregional

- **ALA (American Library Association) JobList**
  http://joblist.ala.org/home/index.cfm?site_id=21926

- **Student Guide: Library and Information Science Jobs Boards**
  http://www.studentguide.org/library-and-information science-jobs-boards

- **LibraryScienceList.com**
  http://librarysciencelist.com

SCHOOLS

- **ALA Accredited Schools**
  www.ala.org/accreditedprograms/directory/alphalist

- **University of Southern Mississippi**
  www.usm.edu/undergraduate
  /library-and-information-science-bs

- **Southern Connecticut State University**
  https://www.southernct.edu/academics/schools/education
  /departments/ils/index.html

- **University of North Texas**
  http://lis.unt.edu

- **Louisiana State University**
  http://www.lsu.edu/chse/slis

■ **University of Pittsburgh**
http://www.ischool.pitt.edu/lis

■ **Wayne State University**
http://slis.wayne.edu/mlis/index.php

■ **University of Arizona**
http://si.arizona.edu/master-arts-library-and-information-science

■ **Indiana University**
www.soic.indiana.edu/graduate/degrees/information-library-science/master-library-science/index.html

■ **University of Buffalo**
http://www.buffalo.edu/gse/online/programs/masters/mls.html

Copyright 2017 Institute For Career Research

Careers Internet Database Website www.careers-internet.org

Careers Reports on Amazon

www.amazon.com/Institute-For-Career-Research/e/B007DO4Y9E

For information please email service@careers-internet.org

TCC South

Crowley Learning Center